Science of the Early Americas

Geraldine Woods

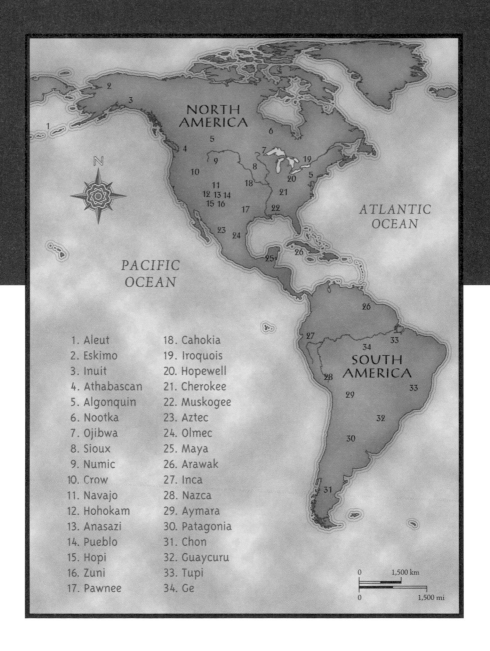

NORTH AMERICA

ATLANTIC OCEAN

PACIFIC OCEAN

SOUTH AMERICA

1. Aleut
2. Eskimo
3. Inuit
4. Athabascan
5. Algonquin
6. Nootka
7. Ojibwa
8. Sioux
9. Numic
10. Crow
11. Navajo
12. Hohokam
13. Anasazi
14. Pueblo
15. Hopi
16. Zuni
17. Pawnee

18. Cahokia
19. Iroquois
20. Hopewell
21. Cherokee
22. Muskogee
23. Aztec
24. Olmec
25. Maya
26. Arawak
27. Inca
28. Nazca
29. Aymara
30. Patagonia
31. Chon
32. Guaycuru
33. Tupi
34. Ge

0   1,500 km

0   1,500 mi

Science of the Early Americas

Geraldine Woods

Science of the Past

FRANKLIN WATTS

A Division of Grolier Publishing
New York • London • Hong Kong • Sydney
Danbury, Connecticut

Photographs ©: Art Resource: 39 (Nicolas Sapieha), 48 (SEF), 13; Ben Klaffke: 37; Corbis-Bettmann: 49 (Burstein Collection), 10, 25; H. Armstrong Roberts,Inc.: 15, 33 (M. Thonig), 38 (K. Scholz), 52 (Foley); James P. Rowan: cover, 27, 28, 35, 42, 54; Marilynn "Angel" Wynn: 11, 23, 51; National Geographic Image Collection: 17 (Stephen L. Alvarez), 30; North Wind Picture Archives: 6, 7, 12, 21, 31; Photo Researchers: 8 (Kenneth Murray), 22 (Soames Summerhays), 34 (Richard J. Green), 40 (Barney McGrath/SPL), 45 (John Sanford); Reinhard Brucker: 19, 41; The Bridgeman Art Library International: 14 (Ms.Palat. 218-220 Book IX Aztec midwife administering herbs to woman after childbirth from an account of Aztec crafts written and illustrated by Bernardino de Sahagun, Spanish, mid 16th century Biblioteca Medicea-Laurenziana,Florence); The Smithsonian Institution: 18; The Time Museum: 53; Tony Stone Images: 36 (Robert Frerck), 43 (James Balog), 44 (Ralph Wetmore), 50 (Alejandro Belaguer), 55 (Larry Olrich), 56 (Chuck Pefley).

Maps created by XNR Productions Inc.
Illustrations by Drew-Brook-Cormack Associates

Library of Congress Cataloging-in-Publication Data

Woods, Geraldine.
      Science of the Early Americas /Geraldine Woods.
          p. cm. — (Science of the past)
      Includes bibliographical references and index.
      Summary: Discusses the scientific accomplishments in such fields as medicine, mathematics, engineering, and astronomy of various groups of American Indians.
      ISBN 0-531-11524-0 (lib. bdg.)   0-516-15941-8 (pbk.)
      1. Science—America—History—Juvenile literature. 2. Science, Ancient— Juvenile literature. 3. Indians—Juvenile literature. [1. Science—History. 2. Science, Ancient. 3. Indians.] I. Title. II. Series.
Q126.4.W66   1999
509.7—dc21   97-44047
                                                    CIP
                                                    AC

CONTENTS

chapter 1

The Birth of American Science

Before settling down in villages, early Americans moved from place to place in search of food. This painting shows Plains Indians skinning an animal and cooking a meal.

For thousands of years, Native Americans lived by hunting wild animals and gathering plants—a kind of lifestyle that demanded constant traveling. When food ran out in one area, the people simply moved to a new location.

About 10,000 years ago, ancient Americans began to grow maize (corn) and other crops. This allowed them to settle permanently in one place. And once they developed a system for dividing work, the people found they had some free time. They began to study and think about the world around them. American science was born.

Early Native Americans harvesting corn

Thousands of years ago, ancient Incan people lived in mountainside cities. Today, all that remains of this great civilization is ruins.

When European explorers arrived in the Americas, they found lands that had already seen the rise (and sometimes the fall) of powerful *civilizations*. The Cahokia, who lived in what is now the midwestern United States, and the Hohokam, who lived in what is now the southwestern United States, were the most important ancient *cultures* in North America, but hundreds of smaller groups also lived in what are now Canada and the United States. There were the Cherokee and the Crow, the Pueblo and the Pawnee, the Anasazi and the Aleut, and many others. This book provides a general overview of all the cultures and highlights some of their most significant scientific accomplishments.

The ancient empires of the Southern Hemisphere are easier to describe because they were larger and more centralized. The Olmec established the first major civilization in what is now Mexico and Central America. They were followed by the Inca in South America, the Maya in Central America, the Aztec in Mexico, and others.

Each of the early American cultures faced a very different climate and geography. North Americans lived in the frozen lands of the far North, the hot deserts of the Southwest, the Northeastern woodlands, and the grasslands of the Great Plains.

Central and South Americans inhabited lowland swamps, the Andes Mountains, the Caribbean Islands, the rain forests, and the deserts. To survive, the ancient Native Americans had to understand their environment. Many achievements in medicine, mathematics, engineering, and astronomy arose from the attempts of these ancient peoples to make use of, and protect themselves from, the natural world.

A Mayan manuscript

We are just now discovering the extent of those achievements. For a long time, historians looked only at what was missing in ancient America. This is partly because all they had to work with were descriptions written by the first European settlers. The people who wrote these descriptions saw the early Americans as primitive. Because their culture was very different, the ancient Americans were thought to be inferior.

Historians had to rely on these biased views because the first peoples of North America had no written languages, and almost all the documents of early people living in Central and South America were burned by European conquerors. No one understood what was left of the complicated writing of the Maya. While *archaeologists* were able to study many of the buildings and artifacts left behind by the ancient Egyptians and other early cultures, this was not possible in the Americas. Many structures and objects had been made of wood, so they decayed over time. And, of course, European settlers often built on top of, or paved over, what was left behind by the early Native Americans. For a long time, the cultures, traditions, and accomplishments of the ancient Americans remained a mystery.

In recent years, however, archaeologists have begun to decode the ancient Mayan writing, and they have made progress in understanding the meaning of many Native American buildings, objects, pictures, and carvings. They have also asked modern Native Americans for assistance. Many groups have kept ancient traditions alive and passed their knowledge from generation to generation in the form of ceremonies, stories, and teachings. By studying all this evidence, we are finally coming to appreciate the science of the early Americas.

Many modern Native Americans, such as this member of the Sioux tribe, keep ancient traditions alive.

This medicine man waits to see how
a patient will respond to treatment.

any early Americans believed that people must achieve *harmony* within themselves and between themselves and the world around them. They believed that sickness resulted from a break in the harmony of the universe.

A healer's goal was to restore balance and harmony with a mixture of the supernatural and the scientific. "Medicine men" were generally religious leaders who gave sick patients drugs or other forms of treatment. In addition, they prayed or performed rituals. In many societies, female elders—whose knowledge of plants had been handed down for generations—treated day-to-day ailments and acted as *midwives.*

This portrait of a Native American healer hangs in the National Museum of American Art in Washington, D.C.

Nature's Pharmacy

A Cherokee legend tells of a time when many animals felt threatened by people. The animals had always been hunted, but as the human population grew, people gained an unfair advantage over other animals. To save themselves, the animals created diseases. The plants, however, felt sorry for the sick and dying people, so each plant offered humans a different kind of medicine.

Aztec healers often treated patients with herbs.

This story shows the importance of plants in Native American health care. Throughout the early Americas, people used tens of thousands of plant remedies. Some were not effective. Tobacco smoke, for example, was actually considered a cure for disease! Today, we know that tobacco smoke causes, rather than cures, diseases. Many plants were prescribed for an illness simply because their appearance matched the ailment. The plants were given names to show their use—snakeroot for snakebite, wormroot for worms, bloodroot to prevent bleeding, and so forth.

Other medicines made from plants were very effective, however. Willow tree bark, for example, was used to reduce a fever. Willows contain salicylic acid—the primary ingredient in one of today's leading fever treatments, aspirin. Patients with heart trouble were treated with the foxglove plant, a source of a modern heart drug called digitalis. Early Native Americans also used the bark of the chinchona tree to treat *malaria*. Today, quinine from the chinchona tree is still used to treat this deadly disease.

Although early Native Americans had never heard of vitamin C, they knew how to obtain and use it for the treatment of scurvy, an illness caused by a lack of that vitamin. In what is now the southwestern United States, vitamin C was obtained from the agave plant. In Canada, early Americans cured scurvy with a mixture of boiled sap and tree bark.

Ancient Peruvians chewed coca leaves or brewed coca tea for energy and mild pain relief.

Early Americans knew the power of foxglove. Today, it is used to make digitalis, a medication given to patients with heart conditions.

Coca is the plant from which cocaine is made. Some Native Americans used plants for birth control, to speed childbirth, and to ease labor pains. Many groups knew of *fungi* or *molds* that cured infections. These life forms are natural sources of the *antibiotics* we use today.

Native American Herbal Remedies

PLANT	USE	INDIAN GROUP
Agave	Scurvy	Southwestern culture
Arrowroot	Smallpox	Arawak, Maya
Cayenne pepper	Eye or ear pain	Maya
Cedar	Diarrhea	Canadian groups
Datayra	Pain relief, cuts	Californian groups
Dogwood	Fever	Many groups
Elderberries	Cause sweating	Iroquois
Green hellebore	Wounds, toothache	Northeastern cultures
Ipecac	Causes vomiting	Many groups
Maguey	Wound dressing	Aztec
May apple	Causes vomiting	Many groups
Mesquite	Eyewash, stomach pain	Southwestern groups
Molle tree	Swelling, wounds	Inca
Nettle	Nosebleed	Aztec
Nopal	Burns	Aztec
Oak bark (green)	Wound dressing	Southwestern cultures
Pennyroyal	Congestion	Aztec
Poplar	Ear pain	Ojibwa
Sassafras	Fever; tonic	North American groups
Sweetgum	Kills germs; stimulant	Many groups
Thimbleberry leaves	Tonic	Northwestern cultures
Valerian root	Stimulant	Aztec
Witch hazel	Dry skin	Mohawk

First Aid

Despite their many successes with plants, most early Native Americans understood only a little about the way the human body functions. Some groups were familiar with the appearance of the body's internal organs. The Inca, for example, mummified their dead. By removing internal organs, they gained some knowledge of the body's structure. As part of a religious ritual, the Aztec cut into a living body and removed the heart. Of course the victim died, but the priests did have a chance to observe the breathing lungs and circulating blood for a few moments.

Most healers probably learned about the body when someone was wounded. Almost all cultures were skilled in setting broken bones, and the Aztec even knew how to make plaster casts. The Plains Indians used

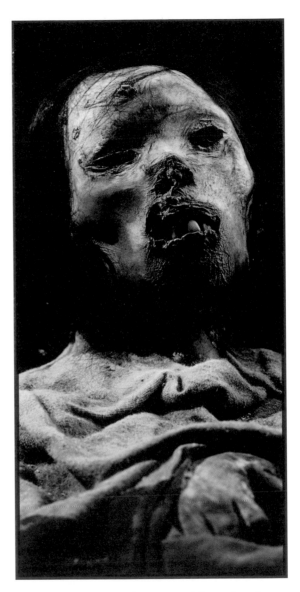

This mummy was discovered by scientists working at an ancient Inca settlement.

a pulley system to put dislocated shoulders back into place. A rope was tied to the patient's arm and then draped over a tree. By pulling on the

This Incan healer is cutting open a patient's skull to relieve pressure on the brain.

rope, the healer forced the arm into the right position. The Inca amputated limbs and made holes in patients' skulls to relieve pressure on the brain. The holes were later covered with silver plates—if the patient lived long enough. Aztec healers treated wounds with hot urine (urine contains no germs) and often cut infected areas open, so they could drain.

Other Treatments and Tools

Many early cultures in North America, particularly in the Southwest, believed that sweating helped the body to rid itself of impurities. (This idea is supported by some doctors today.) To encourage sweating, some groups built "sweat lodges"—small, usually round buildings that could be heated to high temperatures. Often, as part of a sacred ritual, a person spent several hours meditating in the sweat lodge. The heat of the sweat lodge was also a favored treatment for arthritis and muscle pains.

Early Central and South Americans who lived near volcanoes performed surgery with knives made from a volcanic glass called *obsidian*. Obsidian can be split so that it has extremely sharp, thin edges. The Aztec stitched wounds with human hair and bone needles. Ancient Native Americans invented the

A Navajo sweat lodge

syringe, a device used for injecting liquid medicine. Some syringes were made out of animal bladders and hollow bones. The Arawak created rubber from tree sap and used it to make syringes.

Many groups knew how to treat snakebites with a *tourniquet*. A tourniquet is a strip of rope or cloth tied tightly around some part of the body, usually an arm or a leg. The tourniquet cuts off the blood flow and keeps the poison in one small area of the body. The healer sucked the poison out of the bite and spat it out before removing the tourniquet. Tourniquets were also used to stop bleeding, as they are today.

Dentistry

The Aztec were proud of their clean, shining teeth. They brushed them with a mixture of salt and powdered charcoal. After they had scraped the *tartar* off, they polished each tooth with white ashes and honey. Ancient Peruvians rubbed their teeth with a plant called "balsam of Peru." In North America, the Meskwakis cleaned their teeth with white clay.

The ancient Maya made dental fillings with jade, turquoise, or gold. However, they considered the fillings as a type of decorative jewelry, not dental care! Many Native Americans treated gum infections by cutting into the painful area, allowing it to drain, and then searing it with heat. The ancients also pulled out decayed teeth with bone tweezers or other tools. Many North American groups treated dental pain with the bark of the prickly ash, which European settlers later named the "toothache tree." Many other plants were made into teas or prepared as hot dressings and then used to relieve mouth pain.

Europe Brings Disease

The first explorers from Europe frequently wrote about the good health of the Native Americans they encountered. However, contact with people from Europe soon proved deadly for the inhabitants of the Americas. Measles, chicken pox, and other illnesses that infected, but seldom killed, Europeans swept through the Native American population.

Why did these diseases kill so many Native Americans? Many diseases are passed from *domesticated* animals to humans. For centuries, Europeans

European diseases killed thousands of early Americans.

had bred and cared for horses, cows, and many other animals. During this time, the Europeans built up *resistance* to the animals' germs. In the Americas, however, these beasts were previously unknown, and so were the diseases they spread. Native Americans had no resistance to the new infections—and no cures. The "gift of the plants" could not save great numbers of ancient Americans from the deadly invasion of European diseases.

An Inuit man ready to face a long,
hard winter

An Inuit man was once asked how he counted. One hand is five, two hands are ten, and each foot adds another five, he explained. The number 20 is one person. A person and a hand is 25. A person and two hands is 30. One hundred is five people or a bundle of fur skins because, according to Inuit custom, skins are always tied in groups of 100.

The Inuit counting system, like many early counting systems, is based on body parts. Other early Americans counted with pebbles, grains of maize, or cocoa beans. Some kept track of numbers with notched sticks or by carving lines in a rock.

The Santa Barbara tribe counted by fours. The number 12, for example, was expressed as 3 fours, and 15 was 3 fours plus another 3. In most counting systems, including ours, 10 is the most important number. The Zuni word for 10 means "all the fingers." "Two times all the fingers" is 20. One hundred is "the fingers times all the fingers."

Some early Americans kept track of time or their harvest by writing numeric symbols on rocks.

The Quipu and the Abacus

Early North Americans knew how to do *arithmetic*. They could add, subtract, divide, and multiply. They did not, however, have a formal system of mathematics. In Central and South America, mathematics was more developed. Both Incan and Mayan mathematics recognized *place value*.

Place value means that the position of the numerals determines their value. In the "Arabic" counting system we use today, we know that 456 is smaller than 654 even though both numbers use the same three symbols. In the number 456, 4 is in the hundreds position, 5 is in the tens position, and 6 is in the units position. In 654, 6 is in the hundreds position, 5 is in the tens position, and 4 is in the units position.

Place value makes arithmetic easier because it is possible to write any number using just a few symbols. Our counting system uses just ten numeric symbols (1, 2, 3, 4, 5, 6, 7, 8, 9, and 0). Place value also allows us to break complex math problems into smaller parts. To add 456 and 654, for example, you add the units (6 + 4), then the tens (5 + 5), and then the hundreds (4 + 6).

Incan numbers were not written. They were recorded on long pieces of colored rope. A collection of knotted ropes tied to one main cord was called a *quipu*. Quipus were like today's computer hard drives. The cord was like a file; the pieces of rope tied onto the cord were like "subfiles." Pieces of rope could hang down from the main cord or extend upward. Knots in the pieces of rope represented numbers. Knots closer to the main cord had higher place values. The knots representing units were farthest from the main cord.

Quipus often contained hundreds of ropes. Besides the position and number of knots, the color of the rope, the type of knot, and the way each rope was tied to the main cord also had meaning. Quipus were public records. For example, the taxes paid by a village, the number of days since the last planting, and other figures were recorded on quipus.

Quipus were probably also used for arithmetic calculations, though no one knows exactly how. The Inca also used a device called the *abacus* as a type of early calculator. Their abacus consisted of a stone box with three levels. Squares and rectangles were carved along each level. Pebbles placed in the squares on the lowest level represented units. When a pebble was moved to a rectangle, it doubled in value. When it was moved to a higher level, it was worth six times as much. By moving pebbles, the Inca could solve math problems.

A representation of a typical quipu

COUNTING SYMBOLS

Arabic	Mayan	Arabic	Mayan
1	•	11	• over bar
2	••	12	•• over bar
3	•••	13	••• over bar
4	••••	14	•••• over bar
5	—	15	two bars
6	• over bar	16	• over two bars
7	•• over bar	17	•• over two bars
8	••• over bar	18	••• over two bars
9	•••• over bar	19	•••• over two bars
10	two bars	0	shell

Mayan Mathematics

The most brilliant mathematicians of the early Americas were the Maya. Their calendar depended on exact, intricate calculations and had its own numerals. Non-calendar numerals were written with three symbols: the dot (units), the bar (fives), and the shell. The shell symbolized zero in most calculations. Other cultures, including the Inca, understood the idea of zero, but the Maya used the zero in more complicated math problems.

Mayan mathematics was based on the numeral 20. Instead of right-to-left place value, they wrote from the bottom to the top, with the higher place value on top of the lower place value. The lowest level counts "ones" up to 19. The next number is written as a dot on the second level (one 20) and a shell on the lowest level (0). A line on the second level stands for five 20s—or 100. The third level is for 400s.

Mayan mathematicians may have used counting boxes to help them do arithmetic. Little bars (fives), cubes (units), and shells (zeros) were probably laid on a carved wooden grid. The lines of the grid helped determine place value.

Weights and Measures

The Ojibwa was a hunting society that lived in what is now Canada. Like most hunters, the Ojibwa had little need for mathematical theory or exact calculations. Their three main measurements for *volume* were based on items

they carried while hunting. Their measurement words have been translated as "hard-containers-full," "backpacks-full," and "soft-containers-full." When the Ojibwa built boats, they measured the wood with their own hands and fingers.

The Inca also based their measurements on body parts. A "hand" was 8 inches (20 cm) long, and a pace was 4 feet (1.2 m) long. Because the Incan civilization was more complex than

Because the Ojibwa were always on the move, they lived in tents that could be easily carried from place to place.

A representation of an Aztec market

that of the Ojibwa, the Inca needed more kinds of measurements. They used the topo (about 6,000 paces) to measure distances traveled, and the fathom, which was equal to 64 inches (160 cm), to measure plots of land. The Inca knew that they could calculate the *area* of a piece of land by multiplying its length and width. They measured quantities of grain in units called "phogca." The Inca also invented a balance scale to weigh gold and silver. Baskets were hung from the ends of a wooden pole. Metal was placed in one basket until it balanced the standard stone weights in the other basket.

The Aztec also used standard measurements. One of the first Spaniards to arrive in Mexico, Bernal Diaz del Castillo, wrote of a great market in the Aztec city of Tlatelolco. Food, cloth, sandals, and other goods were measured using lengths of rope and by standard-size containers. A bin that could hold 200 tons was called a "troje." A "tlacopintli" could hold about 125 pounds (56 kg).

The Aztec also kept very exact measurements of land. One book contains drawings of each family's fields with careful notes on size. Lines and dots along each side of the field show the length. Another symbol shows the area. Some picture symbols represent fractions. Like other Central and South Americans, the Aztec thought of fractions in a different way. We might say that 4 is $\frac{1}{5}$ of 20. The Aztec would have said that you must add 4 five times in order to reach 20.

No one knows how the Aztec calculated area. Like other early American cultures, they left no mathematics textbooks. It is clear, however, that they were skilled at basic mathematics. Otherwise, they would not have been able to build such impressive buildings and irrigation systems. You will learn more about the architectural accomplishments of the Aztec and other ancient American civilizations in the next chapter.

Monk's Mound

Monk's Mound is a huge, flat mound in what is now the midwestern United States. It is about ten stories high and as large as a football field. To build the mound, ancient Americans had to transport a lot of soil to the site—enough to fill about 1,500,000 refrigerators. Monk's Mound was probably built by the Sioux about 1,000 years ago. Archaeologists think it may have been a ceremonial or royal center. Because European settlers mistakenly thought that the mound had been constructed by the Cahokia Indians, they called the entire area "Cahokia." Archaeologists have identified more than 100 mounds in Cahokia. Many of these mounds were once covered with black clay and topped with wooden buildings.

These Hopewell mounds are located in Ohio.

The remains of earthen mounds can be found in other parts of the United States, too. Some were built about 2,000 years ago by a group of people we now call the "Hopewell." No one knows their real name. "Hopewell" is the name of the man who owned the farm where the first mounds were discovered. Most of the Hopewell mounds were burial sites.

This serpent-shaped mound was built by early Americans.

Some mounds are impressive sculptures. In Ohio, a snake 1,300 feet (396 m) long winds through the countryside. Earthen buffalo, deer, dogs, bears, and other animals were also constructed. We know very little about the people who made these mounds, and even less about their building techniques. From the tools they left behind, we know the soil was dug with shells or stone hoes and carried to the mounds in baskets or leather bags. And all the work was done without the help of animals. Ancient North Americans had neither horses nor oxen to pull carts or drag heavy loads.

Stonework

The Maya, Inca, and Aztec built stone step pyramids. The Olmec constructed the Pyramid of the Sun and the Pyramid of the Moon in Teotihuacán, near what is now Mexico City. The Olmec pyramids, which are about 2,000 years old, were constructed around a core of rubble and mud bricks. The pyramids were then coated with white plaster and held in place with outer walls made of stone.

The Olmec Pyramid of the Moon still stands today.

The Anasazi built settlements in rocky cliffs. This one is located in Colorado.

The Mayan temples of Chichén Itzá and the Incan city of Machu Picchu also show the skills of their builders. In North America, the Anasazi carved sandstone into blocks and constructed multistory "apartment houses" on the sides of cliffs. They used a step pattern to create rooftop terraces.

The Inca and Maya were excellent stoneworkers. The Maya invented the *corbeled arch,* which consists of many layers of stone. Each layer extends a little farther inward, gradually narrowing the opening. A flat stone tops off each arch.

This corbeled arch was built by the Maya more than 1,000 years ago.

An example of the Inca's fine stone-work

Creating such an arch demands precision and planning. Before construction began, architects made clay models of each structure. Workers then cut stone from nearby quarries, probably by making small cracks and hammering wedges into them until the rock split. To shape the stone blocks, workers probably rubbed them with harder stones and then sanded them smooth. Each block had to be dragged into position. The early Americans may have used logrollers or wooden sleds to make this part of the job easier.

Incan blocks were so well shaped that they fit together without cement. Some were cut like puzzle pieces, with up to twenty interlocking angles. Incan walls are so sturdy that they fare better than modern buildings during earthquakes!

The Inca also paved about 19,000 miles (30,000 km) of roads to connect their far-flung empire. To cross swampy areas, they created stone causeways (a type of bridge). They also built suspension (hanging) bridges of wood and twisted vines tied to stone towers.

Irrigation and Terrace Farming

The early Americans tried to control their supply of water with irrigation systems. In the southwestern United States, the Hohokam built canals to irrigate their fields. The stone canals were lined with clay to conserve every drop of water. The water system of Phoenix, Arizona, follows the plan of the original Hohokam canals—some of which have been rebuilt and are still in use.

The Inca planned their roads and public water systems carefully. They used clay models to design roads and decide what types of farming improvements were necessary. They also constructed irrigation canals. Ancient Incans even straightened winding rivers and changed the course of streams! The Maya also built reservoirs to hold water, including one that held 32 million gallons (121 million L) of water.

Early American farmers built aqueducts like this one to transport water to their fields.

At one time, the grassy terraces at the bottom of this photograph were used to grow crops.

In mountainous areas, the Inca and Maya constructed a series of terraces, turning steep slopes into wide, flat steps that could be farmed. First, a stone wall was built around a ledge. Loose rubble was placed inside the wall so that extra water could drain. Fertile soil was then added to the terrace, which was now ready for planting. In swampy areas, the Maya designed drainage canals and piled up soil. These raised fields were drier than the swampy ground beneath them.

The Aztec constructed a 10-mile (16-km) dike across Lake Texcoco to protect this source of fresh drinking water. The dike kept out salt water from the ocean. They also built an aqueduct with two channels—one brought clean water into the city while the other was being cleaned. Perhaps the greatest engineering achievement of the Aztec was the *chinampa*.

Chinampas

What do you do when you have a lot of water and not enough farmland? Create artificial islands, or chinampas. Here's how the Aztec did it.

First, workers anchored a reed basket to the bottom of a lake. Next, they filled the basket, which was about 8 feet (2.4 m) wide and 50 feet (15.2 m) long, with water plants and mud from the lake bottom. The workers added fast-growing plants to the center of the basket and planted willow trees around its inside edges. Soon the plants' roots had grown through the basket and into the lake bed. Eventually, the chinampa became dry, solid land, and food crops such as maize, beans, and chilies could be planted.

The areas between chinampas became canals. Farmers could then travel from one chinampa to another by boat. The water level in the canals could be raised or lowered, depending on how much water was needed to irrigate the growing crops.

Ancient Aztecs building a chinampa

chapter 5

Studying the Sky

Early American astronomers
followed the path of the stars
that filled the night sky.

When should the corn be planted? How long until the next rainy season? To answer such questions, early American *astronomers* watched the sun, the planets, and the stars. Since the movement of the stars and planets is predictable, their positions were used to mark the passage of time. Knowledge of astronomy was so important in ancient American cultures that stargazers often served as priests. In some cultures, the king or chief was also the head astronomer.

Archaeologists have discovered a great deal of evidence suggesting that early Americans took stargazing very seriously. In Chaco Canyon, New Mexico, the Anasazi carved notches into stone to mark the sunrise at the summer and winter *solstices* (the longest and shortest days of the year). The ancient Navajo painted star maps and planted their crops when one particular *constellation* appeared parallel to the horizon in the early evening. In

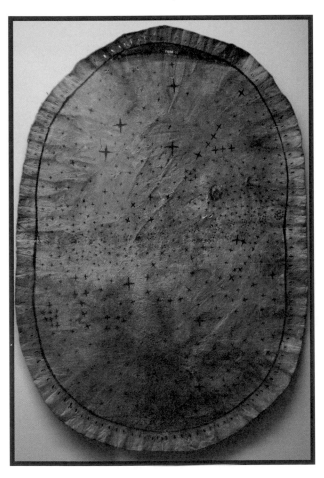

A Pawnee star map

The ancient Mayan people may have used El Caracol as an observatory.

Nazca, Peru, long lines scratched into the desert mark the position of the rising sun at the solstices. Large animal figures, also drawn on the desert floor, may have symbolized the constellations.

In the Mayan city of Chichen Itzá, a tall, round tower called El Caracol may have served as an observatory. Mayan paintings show astronomers measuring the distance between stars with a pair of crossed sticks. These sophisticated people also recorded the phases of Venus, the appearances of *comets,* and the timing of *eclipses.* The Maya even calculated the monthly cycle of the moon to within 23 seconds and the solar (sun) year to within $1/5,000$ of a second!

The Maya kept records of comets and other celestial events.

Measuring Time

Many early Americans used human activities to measure time. The Ojibwa described long periods of time by the number of "sleeps," rather than the number of days. A smaller measure of time was "the pipesmoke"—the amount of time needed to smoke one pipe of tobacco. Most Native Americans divided days into four periods: the time between sunrise and noon, the time between noon and sunset, the time between sunset and midnight, and the time between midnight and the next sunrise. A group in South Carolina determined the time of day by measuring how many "hands" the sun was above the horizon. The Choctaw drew

Many groups of early Americans used the sun's movement to measure time.

44

two parallel lines on the ground. The time it took the sun to cross the lines was an "hour."

A few cultures recorded their knowledge and created calendars. The Nootka of western Canada measured time with "moons" named after the activity that took place during that period. October was the "Time for Splitting and Drying Salmon," and February was "Herring Fishing Moon." The Nootka year was 14 moons long. Each moon lasted about 20 days, but the chiefs could add or take away days, depending on what the group was doing.

The Hopi used features in their landscape, such as mountains or rocks, etc., to follow the rising points of the sun. The view surrounding a village was their calendar. Like the Nootka, the Hopi divided their year into "moons." Each moon was slightly shorter than one of our months. The Hopi added an extra month every 3 years to make the "moon" year correspond to the solar year.

The early Central and South American calendars had many similar features. The most advanced was the Mayan calendar.

The Nootka and Hopi used the moon to measure the passage of time.

The Maya Calendar

The Maya measured time using many different types of calendars. The two most important calendars were the solar calendar and the "sacred" calendar, which could be used together. The solar calendar was based on the length of time it takes Earth to circle the sun. The Mayan solar year was 365 days long and divided into 18 months—each with 20 days—for a total of 360 days. The 5 extra days, which were considered unlucky, were called "the sleep."

The Mayan sacred year was 260 days long. (That number may have been chosen because it is close to the length of a human pregnancy.) The sacred year was divided into 20 weeks, and each week was 13 days long. To identify a specific day, the Maya used a name and a number: "1 Alligator," "2 Wind," "3 House," and so on. They went in order through the names of the days and the numbers 1 to 13. On the fourteenth day, they used the fourteenth name but went back to the number one. After the twentieth name, they returned to the first name. The name-number combinations came back to "1 Alligator" every 260 days.

The two Mayan calendars could be used together. A day might be called "1 House 2 Wind." The "1 House" would represent the day on the solar calendar, and the "2 Wind" would represent the day on the sacred calendar. Using this system, it took 52 years for all the combinations to pass.

The Maya also kept a "long count" calendar with units of 20 days, 360 days, 7,200 days, 144,000 days, and even higher amounts. The long count calendar told the Maya how much time had passed since the starting date, just as our years do. Yet another calendar, the "short count," kept time with 7,200-day unit.

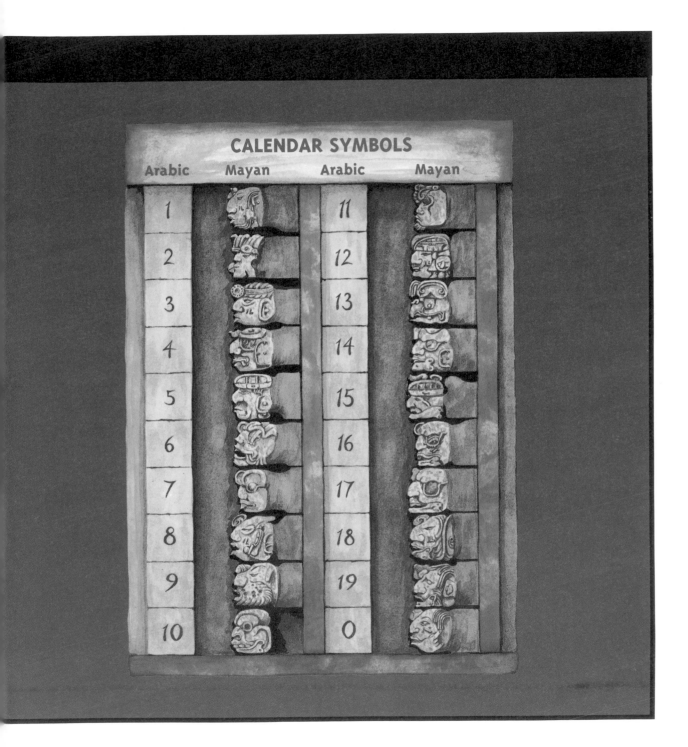

Building According to the Stars

The early Americans recorded much of their astronomical knowledge on the walls of buildings. The Mayan El Castillo pyramid has seven serpents carved on it. On the autumn *equinox* (the autumn day halfway between the solstices), the sun shines through the mouths of all seven serpents. The Aztec Templo Mayor can be used to sight the sun when it is directly over the *equator,* and the Olmec Pyramids of the Sun and Moon are oriented to the Pleiades, a cluster of stars in the constellation Taurus.

El Castillo pyramid was built by Maya living on Mexico's Yucatan Peninsula.

Ancient Pawnee houses were placed so that the rising sun at the equinox would shine through the doorway onto an altar.

In northwest Mexico, many ancient structures were built to align with the rising or setting sun at the solstices. So were some of the Cahokia mounds. The center line of Pottery Mound, for example, points to the location of sunrise on the winter solstice and sunset on the summer solstice.

Near Cahokia, archaeologists have found the remains of a structure they call Woodhenge. It is about 1,000 years old and consists of 48 equally spaced wooden posts arranged in a circle that is 410 feet (125 m) across.

The ruins of Cuzco, an Incan city

Remains of the Big Horn Medicine Wheel in Wyoming

Four of the posts mark north, south, east, and west. Woodhenge may have been used to determine the timing of the solstices and the equinoxes.

Pillars surrounding Cuzco, an Incan city, may have been used as a type of calendar. According to one historian, when the sun passed the first pillar, it was time to plant crops in the nearby mountains. When the sun passed another pillar, it was time to plant crops in nearby valleys.

A giant stone structure in Wyoming is known as the Big Horn Medicine Wheel. It is about 75 feet (23 m) wide and looks like a bicycle wheel lying on its side. Some spokes of the wheel-shaped structure line up with the position of sunrise on the summer solstice. Others mark the pre-dawn positions of three stars that rise 1 month apart. The rising of the last star, Sirius, warned the early Americans that winter would soon arrive. Similar medicine wheels can be found in Montana and Canada.

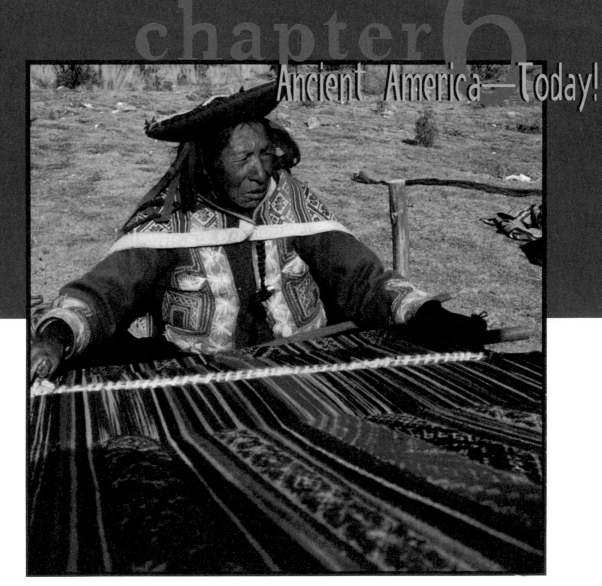

A Peruvian woman weaving in the
same way that Incan people did
thousands of years ago.

A Mayan woman sits on the ground outside her house. A loom is strapped to her back, and she is weaving cloth in a pattern that identifies her village. Although the woman is alive today and may even be weaving as you read this book, she uses the same type of loom and the same pattern that her ancestors used 1,000 years ago. Many of the tools and devices created by the early Americans are still used today.

In some parts of the Andes Mountains, shepherds still keep track of their herds using quipus—just as the ancient Inca did thoudsands of years ago. People living in many parts of South and Central America still water their crops using irrigation systems designed and built by Incan, Mayan, or Aztec engineers.

Not all quipus had a main cord. Some, like this one, radiated out from a central point.

An ear of early corn was probably no bigger than a walnut. Early Americans carefully bred them to create a number of larger, more nutritious varieties.

The greatest achievement of early American agriculture is the plants themselves. Native Americans domesticated 60 percent of the crops grown around the world today. These include squash, corn, peanuts, potatoes, peppers, and beans. One of today's most important non-food plants—the rubber tree—was first identified by Native Americans.

Ancient American astronomy also survives. Many groups still follow the sun's passage across the sky and mark the solstices. In one area of

Guatemala, the Chorti Maya mark the passage of the sun in relation to landscape features. In the southwestern United States, some Hopi tell time by studying shadows cast by the sun. These peoples have found ways to integrate their cultural history with the modern world. Although they use ancient methods to measure time, most also wear wristwatches and have clocks in their homes.

Taking the best from the past and the present is also common in Native American medicine. An ailing Navajo might visit a healer who will prescribe herbs and perform a special ceremony to restore mental, phys-

Some early Americans ate agave plants to prevent scurvy.

ical, and spiritual harmony. If the Navajo decided to go to a doctor, the physician might prescribe medicine based on a Native American discovery. About 200 Native American drugs are now recognized as safe and effective medicines. The Native American remedy for diabetes and the drug they use as birth control have the same basic ingredients as modern medications for the same purposes.

The European explorers thought of themselves as the carriers of ideas from their continent to the Americas. Now we know that information traveled in both directions. As archaeologists continue their study of the ancient Americas, they will probably discover even more contributions from Native American scientists.

The peoples living in the Americas before European settlers arrived had advanced civilizations. Many groups had systems for counting and measuring. They also knew how to use the movements of the sun, planets, and moon to record the passage of time. They even understood how plants could be used to heal the sick.

GLOSSARY

abacus—a counting frame used by a number of civilizations since ancient times. It can be used to rapidly add and subtract numbers and perform other mathematical calculations.

antibiotic—a medication used to fight an infection caused by bacteria.

archaeologist—a scientist who studies past human life and activities.

area—the amount of space within an established set of lines.

arithmetic—basic mathematical calculations, such as addition, subtraction, multiplication, and division.

astronomer—a scientist who studies stars and planets.

chinampa—the Aztec name for an artificial island in the middle of a lake.

civilization—the culture of people living in a particular area during a specific period of time.

corbeled arch—a type of support structure invented by the Maya. Other types of arches were developed by the Romans. Roman arches were used in the construction of great aqueducts, bridges, and arenas.

comet—a ball of rock and ice that travels through space.

constellation—a group of stars in a specific area of the sky.

culture—an organized way of life established by a group of people who live together.

diabetes—a medical condition in which the body fails to use sugar properly.

domesticate—to tame a wild animal as a pet or to keep for food.

eclipse—a phenomenon that occurs when an object is blocked by something else. During a solar eclipse, the moon passes between the sun and Earth. As a result, the sun cannot be seen for several minutes. During a lunar eclipse, Earth passes between the sun and the moon and casts a shadow over the moon.

equator—an imaginary line that runs around Earth's center. Everything south of the equator is called the Southern Hemisphere, and everything to the north of it is called the Northern Hemisphere.

equinox—the two times of the year when the sun is over the equator and day and night are exactly equal in length. The autumn equinox occurs in September, and the spring equinox occurs in March.

fungus (pl. fungi)—a group of creatures that includes mushrooms and toadstools, yeasts, and molds. Some fungi can cause sickness; others can cure some types of infections.

harmony—agreement.

midwife (pl. midwives)—a person who assists during childbirth.

malaria—a disease spread by mosquitoes.

mold—a life form that breaks down other creatures when they die. Molds are used in some types of medications.

obsidian—a dark natural glass that forms when lava cools.

place value—the value given to a digit as a result of its position in a number. In 71, the place value of 7 is tens. In 718, the place value of 7 is hundreds.

quipu—a device used by the Inca to record numbers and perform simple mathematical calculations.

resistance—the ability to fight off an infection caused by either a virus or a bacterium.

solstice—the shortest and longest days of the year. The summer solstice marks the longest day of the year in the Northern Hemisphere and the shortest day of the year in the Southern Hemisphere. The winter solstice marks the shortest day of the year in the Northern Hemisphere and the longest day of the year in the Southern Hemisphere.

spoke—one of the small bars that radiates from the center point of some types of wheels. A bicycle wheel has spokes.

tartar—a mixture of food particles and saliva that builds up on teeth.

tourniquet—a device used to stop blood flow.

volume—the amount of space occupied by an object.

RESOURCES

Books

Bancroft Hunt. *The Indians of the Great Plains.* New York: Peter Bedrick Books, 1989.

Baquedano, Elizabeth. *Aztec, Inca, and Maya.* Eyewitness Books, New York: Alfred A. Knopf, 1993.

Griffin-Pierce, Trudy. *The Encyclopedia of Native America.* New York: Viking, 1995.

Hooper Trout, Lawana. *The Maya.* New York: Chelsea House, 1991.

Kendall, Sarita. *The Incas.* New York: Macmillan, 1992.

Warburten, Lisa. *Aztec Civilization.* San Diego: Lucent Books, 1995.

Westerheim, Margo. *Calendars of the World.* Oxford: Oneworld, 1993.

White, John Manchip. *North American Indians.* London: BT Batsford Ltd., 1979.

Videos

Myths and Moundbuilders. PBS Home Video, 1981.

Spirit of the Jaguar. PBS Home Video, 1997.

Internet Sites

For information on the Moundbuilders, try this site: **http://medicine. wustl.edu/~~kellerk/cahokia.html.**

This site has an extensive list of links that will take you to information about the Anasazi, Inca, Maya, Aztec, Cahokia, and other groups of early Americans. It can be reached at **http://www.netaxs.com/~bampolsk/ mesoarch.html.**

Links to the Past, which was developed by the U.S. National Parks Service has information about various groups of Native Americans that lived in North America. Its address is **http://www.cr.nps.gov/.**

For information on early Mexico, try this site: **http://www.msstate.edu:80/ archives/history/Latin_America/Mexico/mexico.html.**

INDEX

ABOUT THE AUTHOR

Geraldine Woods is the author of more than thirty-five books for young people. One of these books, Science in Ancient Egypt, is also part of the Science of the Past series published by Franklin Watts. Many of her other books were written with her husband, Harold. Ms. Woods also teaches English and directs the independent study program at the Horace Mann School in New York City. The Woodses have one son, Thomas, who is now in law school.